How to be successful in affiliate marketing business as a beginner

A Comprehensive Guide to Building a Profitable Online Business from Scratch

David A. Miller

All rights reserved. No part of this publication may
be reproduced,
distributed, or transmitted in any form or by any
means, including
photocopying, recording, or other electronic or
mechanical methods,
without the prior written permission of the
publisher, except in the case
of brief quotations embodied in critical reviews and
certain other
noncommercial uses permitted by copyright law.
Copyright ©David A. Miller, 2024.

ACKNOWLEDGE

I would like to express my sincere gratitude to the organization for their invaluable support and guidance throughout the writing of this ebook. Their expertise and encouragement have been instrumental in shaping the content and ensuring its quality. I am also deeply thankful to the countless affiliate marketers and industry experts whose insights and experiences have enriched the pages of this book. Finally, I extend my heartfelt appreciation to my readers for their interest and trust in embarking on this affiliate marketing journey together."

Table of Contents

1. **Introduction to Affiliate Marketing**
   What is Affiliate Marketing?
   Why Choose Affiliate Marketing as a Business Model?

2. **Understanding the Basics**
   How Affiliate Marketing Works
   Players in Affiliate Marketing: Merchants, Affiliates, Customers

3. **Choosing Your Niche**
   - Identifying Your Interests and Passions
   - Researching Profitable Niches
   - Assessing Competition and Demand

4. **Building Your Platform**
   - Setting Up a Website or Blog
   - Creating Valuable Content
   - Utilizing Social Media and Other Channels

5. **Finding Affiliate Programs**
   - Researching and Selecting Programs
   - Evaluating Commission Structures and Payout Methods
   - Avoiding Pitfalls and Scams

6. Driving Traffic to Your Offers
- SEO Basics
- Content Marketing Strategies
- Paid Advertising Options

7. Converting Visitors into Customers
- Understanding Audience Needs
- Crafting Effective CTAs
- Building Trust and Credibility

8. Optimizing Your Strategy
- Tracking and Analyzing Results
- Making Data-Driven Decisions
- Scaling Your Business

9. Legal and Ethical Considerations
- Disclosures and Transparency
- Avoiding Unethical Practices
- Staying Compliant with Regulations

10. Case Studies and Success Stories
- Real-World Examples
- Lessons Learned
- Inspiration for Beginners

11. Conclusion
- Recap of Key Takeaways

- Final Tips and Advice

INTRODUCTION

Understanding the Basics of Affiliate Marketing

Affiliate marketing is a dynamic and rapidly growing industry that offers individuals the opportunity to earn income by promoting products or services online. In this section, we'll explore the fundamental principles of affiliate marketing, including how it works, the key players involved, and why it has become such a popular business model.

How Affiliate Marketing Works

At its core, affiliate marketing operates on a simple premise: a merchant rewards affiliates for driving traffic or sales to their products or services. This is typically done through the use of unique tracking links or codes, which allow the merchant to attribute any sales generated by the affiliate's promotional efforts.

Let's break down the process step by step:

1. Affiliate Signs Up: The affiliate joins an affiliate program offered by a merchant or advertiser. This

could be an individual company's in-house program or a third-party affiliate network that connects affiliates with a variety of merchants.

2. Access to Promotional Materials: Once approved, the affiliate gains access to a range of promotional materials, including banner ads, text links, product images, and other marketing assets provided by the merchant.

3. Promotion and Marketing: The affiliate promotes the merchant's products or services through various online channels, such as their website, blog, social media accounts, email newsletters, or YouTube videos. The goal is to attract potential customers and encourage them to click on the affiliate's unique tracking link or code.

4. Tracking and Attribution: When a user clicks on the affiliate's link or code and makes a purchase or performs a desired action (such as signing up for a free trial or filling out a lead form), the affiliate network or tracking software records the transaction and attributes it to the affiliate.

5. Commission Payout: The merchant tracks the affiliate's referrals and calculates the commission owed based on the agreed-upon terms, such as a

percentage of the sale amount or a flat fee per referral. The affiliate receives payment for their efforts, usually on a monthly basis.

Key Players in Affiliate Marketing

Several parties are involved in the affiliate marketing ecosystem, each playing a distinct role:

1. Merchants: Also known as advertisers or vendors, merchants are the companies or individuals who own the products or services being promoted. They create affiliate programs to enlist affiliates to help drive sales and grow their business.

2. Affiliates: Affiliates, also called publishers or partners, are the individuals or entities that promote the merchant's products or services in exchange for a commission. Affiliates can range from individual bloggers and content creators to large media companies and marketing agencies.

3. Customers: Customers are the end-users who purchase the merchant's products or services after being referred by an affiliate. They may be influenced by the affiliate's marketing efforts, such as product reviews, recommendations, or promotional discounts.

4. Affiliate Networks: Affiliate networks act as intermediaries between merchants and affiliates, providing a platform where affiliates can find and join multiple affiliate programs within a single network. They also facilitate tracking, reporting, and commission payments for both parties.

5. Tracking Software: Tracking software is used to monitor and record the activity of affiliates, including clicks, conversions, and commission earnings. It ensures accurate tracking and attribution of sales or leads generated by affiliates' promotional efforts.

Why Affiliate Marketing is Popular

Affiliate marketing has experienced exponential growth in recent years, thanks to several factors that make it an attractive business model:

1. Low Barrier to Entry: Unlike traditional business models that require significant upfront investment and overhead costs, affiliate marketing can be started with minimal financial resources. Affiliates don't need to create their own products or hold inventory, making it accessible to anyone with an

internet connection and a passion for a particular niche.

2. Flexible and Scalable*: Affiliate marketing offers unparalleled flexibility, allowing affiliates to work from anywhere in the world and set their own schedule. Whether you're a full-time parent, student, or professional, you can easily integrate affiliate marketing into your existing lifestyle. Additionally, affiliate marketing is highly scalable, meaning you can grow your income by expanding your audience, diversifying your promotional channels, and partnering with multiple merchants.

3. Passive Income Potential: One of the most appealing aspects of affiliate marketing is its potential to generate passive income. Once you've created and published high-quality content or promotional materials, they can continue to attract visitors and generate revenue for months or even years to come, with minimal ongoing effort required on your part.

4. Diverse Monetization Opportunities: Affiliate marketing offers a wide range of monetization opportunities across virtually every niche and industry imaginable. Whether you're passionate about health and wellness, technology, finance,

fashion, or travel, there are affiliate programs available to suit your interests and cater to your audience's needs.

5. Performance-Based Rewards: Unlike traditional advertising models where you pay upfront for exposure regardless of results, affiliate marketing operates on a performance-based model. Affiliates only earn commissions when they successfully drive a desired action, such as a sale, lead, or click, incentivizing them to focus on driving high-quality traffic and maximizing conversions.

In conclusion, affiliate marketing is a dynamic and rewarding business model that offers individuals the opportunity to earn income by promoting products or services online. By understanding how affiliate marketing works, the key players involved, and the reasons for its popularity, you'll be well-equipped to embark on your own affiliate marketing journey and unlock the endless possibilities it offers for financial success and personal fulfillment.

CHAPTER 2:

Understanding the Basics of Affiliate Marketing

Affiliate marketing has emerged as one of the most popular and effective ways to monetize online content. Whether you're a blogger, social media influencer, or website owner, affiliate marketing offers a flexible and lucrative opportunity to earn commissions by promoting products or services to your audience. In this comprehensive guide, we'll explore the fundamental concepts of affiliate marketing, including how it works, the key players involved, and strategies for success.

1. What is Affiliate Marketing?

Affiliate marketing is a performance-based marketing strategy where affiliates (publishers) promote products or services on behalf of merchants (advertisers) and earn a commission for each sale, lead, or action generated through their referral. It operates on a revenue-sharing model, with affiliates receiving compensation based on the desired outcome, such as a completed purchase or a sign-up.

2. How Does Affiliate Marketing Work?

The affiliate marketing process typically involves the following steps:

Affiliate Sign-Up: Affiliates join affiliate programs offered by merchants or affiliate networks. They receive unique tracking links or codes to track their referrals accurately.

- Product Promotion: Affiliates promote the merchant's products or services through various channels, including their website, blog, social media platforms, email newsletters, and YouTube videos. They create compelling content to attract and engage their audience.

- User Clicks on Affiliate Link*: When a user clicks on the affiliate's tracking link or code and makes a purchase or performs a desired action (e.g., signing up for a free trial), the affiliate is credited with the referral.

- Tracking and Attribution: Affiliate networks or tracking software record the user's activity and attribute the referral to the affiliate who generated the click. This ensures accurate tracking of conversions and commissions.

- Commission Payout*: The merchant calculates the affiliate's earnings based on the agreed-upon commission structure and payout terms. Affiliates receive payments for their referrals, usually on a monthly basis.

3. Key Players in Affiliate Marketing

Several parties are involved in the affiliate marketing ecosystem:

- Merchants/Advertisers: Companies or individuals that own the products or services being promoted. They create affiliate programs to enlist affiliates to help drive sales and increase brand awareness.

- Affiliates/Publishers: Individuals or entities that promote the merchant's products or services in exchange for a commission. Affiliates can be bloggers, influencers, content creators, website owners, or social media personalities.

- Customers: End-users who purchase the merchant's products or services after being referred by an affiliate. They may be influenced by the affiliate's promotional content, such as product reviews, recommendations, or special offers.

- Affiliate Networks: Intermediaries that connect merchants with affiliates and facilitate the affiliate marketing process. They provide a platform where affiliates can find and join multiple affiliate programs, access promotional materials, and track their performance.

- Tracking Software: Tools and software used to track and monitor the activity of affiliates, including clicks, conversions, and commission earnings. Tracking software ensures accurate attribution of sales or leads generated by affiliates' promotional efforts.

4. Why Affiliate Marketing is Popular

Affiliate marketing has gained widespread popularity for several reasons:

- Low Barrier to Entry: Unlike traditional business models that require significant upfront investment and overhead costs, affiliate marketing can be started with minimal financial resources. Affiliates don't need to create their own products or hold inventory, making it accessible to anyone with an internet connection and a passion for a particular niche.

- Flexible and Scalable: Affiliate marketing offers unparalleled flexibility, allowing affiliates to work from anywhere in the world and set their own schedule. Whether you're a full-time parent, student, or professional, you can easily integrate affiliate marketing into your existing lifestyle. Additionally, affiliate marketing is highly scalable, meaning you can grow your income by expanding your audience, diversifying your promotional channels, and partnering with multiple merchants.

- Passive Income Potential: One of the most appealing aspects of affiliate marketing is its potential to generate passive income. Once you've created and published high-quality content or promotional materials, they can continue to attract visitors and generate revenue for months or even years to come, with minimal ongoing effort required on your part.

- Diverse Monetization Opportunities: Affiliate marketing offers a wide range of monetization opportunities across virtually every niche and industry imaginable. Whether you're passionate about health and wellness, technology, finance, fashion, or travel, there are affiliate programs available to suit your interests and cater to your audience's needs.

- Performance-Based Rewards: Unlike traditional advertising models where you pay upfront for exposure regardless of results, affiliate marketing operates on a performance-based model. Affiliates only earn commissions when they successfully drive a desired action, such as a sale, lead, or click, incentivizing them to focus on driving high-quality traffic and maximizing conversions.

5. Conclusion

In conclusion, affiliate marketing is a dynamic and rewarding business model that offers individuals the opportunity to earn income by promoting products or services online. By understanding how affiliate marketing works, the key players involved, and the reasons for its popularity, you'll be well-equipped to embark on your own affiliate marketing journey and unlock the endless possibilities it offers for financial success and personal fulfillment.

This guide provides a comprehensive overview of the basics of affiliate marketing, from its core principles to its practical applications in today's digital landscape. Whether you're a beginner looking to get started or an experienced affiliate marketer seeking to refine your strategies, mastering the fundamentals is essential for long-term success in this dynamic industry.

CHAPTER 3:
Choosing Your Niche in Affiliate Marketing

Selecting the right niche is crucial to your success as an affiliate marketer. Your niche determines the audience you target, the products you promote, and ultimately, the profitability of your affiliate marketing business. In this comprehensive guide, we'll explore the importance of choosing the right niche, strategies for identifying profitable niches, and tips for evaluating competition and demand.

1. Why Your Niche Matters

Your niche is the specific topic, industry, or subject area that you focus on in your affiliate marketing efforts. It's essential to choose a niche that aligns with your interests, expertise, and audience's needs for several reasons:

- *Passion and Knowledge: Selecting a niche that you're passionate about or knowledgeable in makes it easier to create high-quality content and engage with your audience authentically. Your enthusiasm for the topic will shine through in your promotional efforts, increasing your credibility and trustworthiness as an affiliate.

- Audience Targeting: Choosing a niche allows you to target a specific audience with common interests and needs. By catering to a niche audience, you can create targeted content that resonates with their preferences, increasing the likelihood of conversions and sales.

- Monetization Opportunities: Certain niches may offer more lucrative monetization opportunities than others. By selecting a niche with high demand and purchasing intent, you can capitalize on affiliate programs with generous commissions and high-converting products or services.

2. Strategies for Identifying Profitable Niches

When choosing your niche, consider the following strategies to identify profitable opportunities:

Personal Interests and Passions: Start by brainstorming topics that align with your personal interests, hobbies, or passions. What topics do you enjoy learning about or discussing? Your enthusiasm for the niche will fuel your motivation and creativity as an affiliate marketer.

- Market Research: Conduct thorough market research to identify niches with sufficient demand and profitability. Use keyword research tools, industry reports, and online forums to explore popular topics, trending products, and emerging market trends.

- Competitor Analysis: Analyze your competitors' strategies and performance within various niches to identify gaps or underserved market segments. Look for niches where you can differentiate yourself and provide unique value to your audience.

- Evaluate Profitability: Consider the potential profitability of each niche based on factors such as average commission rates, product pricing, and customer lifetime value. Choose niches with products or services that offer attractive commission structures and recurring revenue opportunities.

3. Assessing Competition and Demand

Once you've identified potential niches, it's essential to assess the level of competition and demand within each niche:

- Keyword Research: Use keyword research tools such as Google Keyword Planner, SEMrush, or Ahrefs to identify relevant keywords and assess search volume and competition levels. Look for long-tail keywords with moderate to high search volume and low competition.

- Content Analysis: Evaluate the quality and quantity of content available within your chosen niche. Are there established authority sites or influencers dominating the niche, or is there room for new players to enter the market? Assess the content gaps and opportunities for differentiation.

- Audience Engagement: Analyze the level of audience engagement and interest within your niche. Are there active online communities, forums, or social media groups discussing topics related to your niche? Engage with your target audience to understand their needs, pain points, and preferences.

- *Product Availability: Consider the availability of affiliate programs and products within your niche.

Are there reputable merchants offering relevant products or services with affiliate programs? Research the commission rates, cookie durations, and promotional resources available to affiliates.

4. Conclusion

Choosing the right niche is a critical step in building a successful affiliate marketing business. By selecting a niche that aligns with your interests, expertise, and audience's needs, you can create valuable content, engage with your audience authentically, and capitalize on lucrative monetization opportunities. Conduct thorough market research, assess competition and demand, and evaluate profitability to identify profitable niches with long-term growth potential. With the right niche, you can lay the foundation for a profitable and sustainable affiliate marketing business.

Chapter 4:
*Building Your Platform in Affiliate Marketing

Your platform serves as the foundation of your affiliate marketing business. It's the digital space where you connect with your audience, create valuable content, and promote affiliate products or services. In this guide, we'll delve into the essential components of building your platform, including setting up a website or blog, creating engaging content, and utilizing various promotional channels.

1. Setting Up Your Website or Blog

A website or blog serves as your central hub for sharing content, engaging with your audience, and promoting affiliate products or services. Follow these steps to set up your platform:

- Choose a Domain Name: Select a memorable and relevant domain name that reflects your niche or brand identity. Consider using keywords related to your niche to improve search engine visibility.

- Select a Web Hosting Provider: Choose a reliable web hosting provider that offers affordable hosting plans, reliable uptime, and excellent customer support. Popular options include Bluehost, SiteGround, and HostGator.

- Install a Content Management System (CMS): Use a CMS like WordPress, Joomla, or Drupal to build and manage your website or blog. WordPress is widely preferred for its ease of use, flexibility, and extensive plugin ecosystem.

- Customize Your Website Design*: Choose a professional and responsive website theme or template that aligns with your niche and branding. Customize the design, layout, and colors to create a visually appealing and user-friendly experience for your visitors.

- *Create Essential Pages*: Set up essential pages such as an About Me/Us page, Contact page, and Privacy Policy page. These pages provide important information about you, your business, and how visitors can get in touch with you.

2. Creating Valuable Content

Compelling content is the cornerstone of your platform's success. Create high-quality, informative, and engaging content that resonates with your audience and addresses their needs and interests. Here are some content ideas to consider:

- Educational Blog Posts: Write in-depth articles, tutorials, guides, and how-to posts that provide valuable insights and solutions to your audience's problems.

- Product Reviews and Recommendations*: Share honest and unbiased reviews of affiliate products or services, highlighting their features, benefits, and potential drawbacks. Include personal experiences and recommendations to help your audience make informed purchasing decisions.

- Visual Content: Incorporate visual elements such as images, infographics, videos, and slideshows to enhance the visual appeal and engagement of your content.

- Case Studies and Success Stories: Showcase real-life examples of how affiliate products or services have helped solve specific problems or achieve desired outcomes for your audience.

- Guest Contributions: Invite guest bloggers, experts, or influencers to contribute guest posts or interviews to your platform, providing fresh perspectives and insights for your audience.

3. Utilizing Social Media and Other Channels

Expand your reach and visibility by leveraging social media platforms and other promotional channels to promote your content and affiliate offers. Here's how:

- Social Media Marketing: Create profiles on popular social media platforms such as Facebook, Instagram, Twitter, LinkedIn, and Pinterest. Share your content, engage with your audience, and promote affiliate products or services through organic and paid social media campaigns.

- Email Marketing: Build an email list of subscribers interested in your niche or content. Send regular newsletters, updates, and promotional offers to nurture relationships with your audience and drive traffic to your platform.

- YouTube Channel: Create video content such as product reviews, tutorials, and demonstrations on YouTube. Optimize your videos for search and include affiliate links in the video descriptions to drive traffic and conversions.

- Podcast: Start a podcast to share valuable insights, interviews, and discussions related to your niche. Monetize your podcast by integrating affiliate promotions and sponsorships into your episodes.

- Forums and Online Communities: Participate in relevant forums, discussion groups, and online communities related to your niche. Share helpful advice, answer questions, and subtly promote your content and affiliate offers where appropriate.

4. Analyzing and Optimizing Performance

Monitor and analyze the performance of your platform using web analytics tools such as Google Analytics. Track key metrics such as website traffic, user engagement, conversion rates, and affiliate link clicks. Use this data to identify areas for improvement and optimize your content and promotional strategies accordingly.

5. Conclusion

Building a successful affiliate marketing platform requires careful planning, strategic execution, and ongoing optimization. By setting up a professional website or blog, creating valuable content, and utilizing various promotional channels, you can attract and engage your audience, drive traffic to your affiliate offers, and ultimately, generate revenue through affiliate commissions. Stay focused on providing value to your audience, adapting to market trends, and continuously improving your platform to achieve long-term success in the competitive world of affiliate marketing.

Chapter 5:
Finding Affiliate Programs

Affiliate programs are the lifeblood of your affiliate marketing business. They provide you with the products or services to promote and offer you the opportunity to earn commissions for your promotional efforts. In this guide, we'll delve into the various methods and strategies for finding affiliate programs that align with your niche, interests, and audience.

1. Researching Affiliate Networks

Affiliate networks are platforms that connect affiliates with merchants offering affiliate programs. They provide a centralized marketplace where you can find a wide range of affiliate programs across various industries and niches. Here are some popular affiliate networks to consider:

- Amazon Associates*: Amazon's affiliate program offers a vast selection of products to promote, making it an excellent choice for affiliate marketers in almost any niche.

- ShareASale*: ShareASale is a leading affiliate network with thousands of merchants and a user-friendly interface that makes it easy to find and join affiliate programs.

- ClickBank: ClickBank specializes in digital products such as ebooks, courses, and software. It's a popular choice for affiliates in niches like health, fitness, self-help, and digital marketing.

- Commission Junction (CJ): CJ Affiliate is one of the largest affiliate networks, featuring a wide range of advertisers and industries. It offers advanced reporting and tracking features for affiliates.

- *Rakuten Advertising (formerly Rakuten LinkShare)*: Rakuten Advertising is another major affiliate network with a global presence and partnerships with top brands and retailers.

- Impact*: Impact is known for its enterprise-level affiliate marketing solutions and partnerships with leading brands in various industries.

2. Exploring Merchant Websites

Many merchants offer affiliate programs directly through their websites. If you have specific brands

32

or products in mind that you'd like to promote, visit their websites and look for affiliate program information in the footer, navigation menu, or dedicated affiliate pages. Some key indicators that a merchant offers an affiliate program include:

- Affiliate or Partner Program*: Look for links or tabs labeled "Affiliate Program," "Partner Program," or "Join Our Team" on the merchant's website.

- Footer Links*: Scroll to the bottom of the website and check the footer for links related to partnerships, affiliates, or business opportunities.

- Contact Information: If you can't find information about an affiliate program on the website, consider reaching out to the merchant directly via email or contact form to inquire about affiliate opportunities.

3. Using Affiliate Directories and Aggregators

Affiliate directories and aggregators compile lists of affiliate programs across various industries and niches, making it easier for affiliates to find and compare programs. These directories often provide detailed information about each program, including commission rates, cookie durations, and promotional resources. Some popular affiliate directories include:

- AffiliatePrograms.com*: AffiliatePrograms.com features a comprehensive directory of affiliate programs categorized by industry and niche, along with reviews and ratings from other affiliates.

-AffiliateSeeking*: AffiliateSeeking offers a searchable database of affiliate programs, affiliate networks, and affiliate resources for affiliates of all experience levels.

- Affiliate Marketing Forum*: Affiliate marketing forums such as Warrior Forum, AffiliateFix, and Digital Point Forum often have dedicated sections or threads where affiliates share information about affiliate programs and network with other affiliates.

*4. Utilizing Search Engines and Social Media

You can also use search engines and social media platforms to find affiliate programs within your niche. Here's how:

- Google Search: Use targeted search queries such as "[Niche] affiliate programs," "[Product/Brand] affiliate program," or "[Industry] partner program" to discover relevant affiliate opportunities.

- Social Media Platforms: Follow brands, companies, and influencers in your niche on social media platforms like LinkedIn, Twitter, and Facebook. Many merchants announce their affiliate programs or partnerships on social media, providing you with opportunities to join.

*5. Evaluating Affiliate Programs

Once you've identified potential affiliate programs, it's essential to evaluate them based on several criteria to ensure they align with your goals and preferences:

- Commission Structure*: Consider the commission rates offered by the affiliate program and whether they are competitive within the industry. Look for programs that offer generous commissions and recurring revenue opportunities.

- Cookie Duration: Check the cookie duration, which determines how long you'll receive credit for a referral after a user clicks on your affiliate link.

Longer cookie durations increase the likelihood of earning commissions from repeat purchases or delayed conversions.

- Product Quality and Relevance: Assess the quality and relevance of the products or services offered by the affiliate program. Choose programs that offer high-quality products that align with your audience's interests and needs.

- Promotional Resources: Look for affiliate programs that provide comprehensive promotional resources such as banners, text links, product images, and landing pages. These resources can help you effectively promote the merchant's products and increase your conversion rates.

- Payment Terms: Review the payment terms, including the payment schedule, minimum payout threshold, and payment methods supported by the affiliate program. Ensure that the payment terms are favorable and align with your financial preferences.

6. Joining and Promoting Affiliate Programs

Once you've selected affiliate programs that meet your criteria, it's time to join and start promoting them to your audience. Here's how to get started:

- Sign Up*: Follow the instructions provided by the affiliate program to sign up and create your affiliate account. Some programs may require approval before you can start promoting their products.

- Access Promotional Materials: Upon approval, access the affiliate dashboard or portal to find promotional materials such as affiliate links, banners, and marketing assets. Customize your affiliate links with tracking parameters to track clicks and conversions accurately.

- Create Content: Develop high-quality content such as blog posts, product reviews, tutorials, videos, or social media posts that promote the merchant's products or services. Incorporate your affiliate links strategically within your content to drive traffic and conversions.

- Promote Across Channels: Promote affiliate products or services across various channels, including your website, blog, social media platforms, email newsletters, YouTube channel, and other promotional channels. Tailor your promotional strategies to each channel and audience to maximize your reach and engagement.

- Monitor Performance: Track and analyze the performance of your affiliate links and promotional efforts using web analytics tools and affiliate tracking software. Monitor key metrics such as clicks, conversions, sales, and commission earnings to assess the effectiveness of your promotional strategies.

7. Conclusion

Finding affiliate programs is a crucial step in building a successful affiliate marketing business. By researching affiliate networks, exploring merchant websites, using affiliate directories, and leveraging search engines and social media platforms, you can discover a wide range of affiliate opportunities within your niche. Evaluate affiliate programs based on criteria such as commission structure, cookie duration, product relevance, and promotional resources to choose programs that align with your goals and preferences. Once you've joined affiliate programs, focus on creating valuable content, promoting affiliate products effectively, and optimizing your promotional strategies to drive traffic, conversions, and revenue.

Chapter 6: Driving Traffic to Your Affiliate Offers

Driving traffic to your affiliate offers is essential for success in affiliate marketing. Without a steady stream of visitors to your content, you won't have anyone to click on your affiliate links or make purchases through your referrals. In this guide, we'll explore various strategies and tactics for driving traffic to your affiliate offers effectively.

1. Search Engine Optimization (SEO)

SEO is a powerful strategy for driving organic traffic to your website or blog. By optimizing your content for search engines, you can attract visitors who are actively searching for information or products related to your niche. Here are some key SEO tactics to implement:

- Keyword Research: Identify relevant keywords and phrases with high search volume and low competition using tools like Google Keyword Planner, SEMrush, or Ahrefs. Target long-tail keywords that are specific to your niche and audience's search intent.

- On-Page Optimization: Optimize your content for target keywords by incorporating them into your page titles, headings, meta descriptions, and body text. Use descriptive and engaging titles and meta descriptions to attract clicks from search engine users.

- Quality Content*: Create high-quality, informative, and engaging content that provides value to your audience. Focus on addressing their questions, solving their problems, and fulfilling their needs with comprehensive and well-researched articles, guides, and tutorials.

-*Link Building: Build backlinks from reputable websites and authority sources within your niche to improve your site's credibility and authority in the eyes of search engines. Focus on acquiring natural, relevant, and high-quality backlinks through guest posting, outreach, and content promotion.

-Site Speed and Mobile Optimization*: Ensure that your website loads quickly and is optimized for mobile devices to provide a seamless user experience. Site speed and mobile-friendliness are important ranking factors that can affect your visibility in search engine results.

*2. Content Marketing

Content marketing is a highly effective strategy for driving traffic and engaging your audience with valuable and relevant content. Here are some content marketing tactics to consider:

-*Blogging*: Create a blog and regularly publish blog posts on topics related to your niche. Share informative articles, how-to guides, product reviews, and industry news to attract and engage your audience.

- Video Marketing: Leverage the power of video content to reach and engage your audience on platforms like YouTube, Vimeo, and social media. Create video tutorials, product demonstrations, reviews, and behind-the-scenes content to showcase affiliate products and provide value to your audience.

- Podcasting: Start a podcast to share insights, interviews, and discussions related to your niche. Publish episodes regularly and promote them through your website, social media, and podcast directories to attract listeners and drive traffic to your affiliate offers.

- Infographics and Visual Content: Create visually appealing and shareable infographics, images, and graphics to convey information and attract attention on social media platforms like Pinterest, Instagram, and Facebook. Visual content can help increase engagement and drive traffic to your website or blog.

- Email Newsletters: Build an email list of subscribers interested in your niche or content. Send regular newsletters containing valuable content, updates, and promotional offers to drive traffic to your affiliate offers and nurture relationships with your audience.

3. Social Media Marketing

Social media platforms offer vast opportunities for driving traffic and promoting affiliate offers to a broad audience. Here's how to leverage social media for affiliate marketing:

- Content Sharing*: Share your blog posts, videos, podcasts, and other content on social media platforms such as Facebook, Twitter, LinkedIn, and Pinterest. Use compelling captions, hashtags, and visuals to attract attention and encourage engagement.

- Community Engagement*: Join relevant groups, forums, and communities on social media platforms where your target audience hangs out. Participate in discussions, answer questions, and provide valuable insights to establish yourself as an authority and build relationships with your audience.

- Influencer Partnerships: Collaborate with influencers and content creators in your niche to reach a larger audience and promote your affiliate offers. Partner with influencers to create sponsored content, co-host events, or run joint promotions to drive traffic and increase conversions.

-*Paid Advertising: Consider investing in paid advertising on social media platforms to reach specific target audiences and drive targeted traffic to your affiliate offers. Experiment with different ad formats, targeting options, and ad creatives to optimize your campaigns for maximum effectiveness.

4. Email Marketing

Email marketing is a powerful strategy for driving traffic and promoting affiliate offers to your subscribers. Here's how to leverage email marketing effectively:

- List Building*: Build an email list of subscribers interested in your niche or content by offering lead magnets, incentives, or exclusive content in exchange for their email addresses. Place opt-in forms on your website, blog, and social media profiles to capture leads.

- Segmentation: Segment your email list based on subscriber preferences, interests, and behaviors to deliver targeted and personalized content. Send relevant offers and recommendations to each segment to maximize engagement and conversions.

-*Automation: Set up automated email sequences, welcome emails, and drip campaigns to nurture relationships with your subscribers and guide them through the customer journey. Use automation tools and platforms like Mailchimp, ConvertKit, or AWeber to streamline your email marketing efforts.

- *Promotional Emails*: Send regular promotional emails containing affiliate offers, product recommendations, discounts, and special promotions to drive traffic and generate sales. Use persuasive copywriting, compelling visuals, and clear calls-to-action to encourage clicks and conversions.

***5. Analyzing and Optimizing Performance**

Monitor and analyze the performance of your traffic-driving strategies using web analytics tools and affiliate tracking software. Track key metrics such as website traffic, engagement metrics, conversion rates, click-through rates, and affiliate commission earnings. Use this data to identify trends, opportunities, and areas for improvement, and optimize your traffic-driving strategies accordingly. Here are some optimization tactics to consider:

- A/B Testing: Experiment with different headlines, content formats, calls-to-action, and promotional strategies to determine which ones resonate best with your audience. Conduct A/B tests to compare variations and optimize for higher conversion rates.

- Conversion Rate Optimization (CRO): Optimize your website or landing pages for conversions by improving usability, design, and user experience. Test different layouts, colors, fonts, and page elements to reduce friction and encourage visitors to take action.

- Keyword Optimization: Continuously monitor and update your keyword targeting strategy based on changes in search engine algorithms, user behavior, and market trends. Optimize your content for new keywords and long-tail variations to capture additional organic traffic.

- Content Updates and Refreshes: Regularly update and refresh your existing content to keep it relevant, accurate, and up-to-date. Add new information, statistics, examples, or case studies to improve its value and appeal to search engines and readers.

- Social Media Engagement: Monitor engagement metrics such as likes, comments, shares, and click-through rates on social media platforms. Analyze which types of content and topics resonate most with your audience and adjust your social media strategy accordingly.

- Email Performance*: Analyze the performance of your email campaigns, including open rates, click-through rates, and conversion rates. Test different subject lines, email formats, and send times to optimize engagement and response rates.

- Affiliate Offer Selection: Continuously evaluate the performance of your affiliate offers and partnerships based on conversion rates, earnings per click (EPC), and return on investment (ROI). Rotate or replace underperforming offers with new opportunities to maximize revenue potential.

6. Conclusion

Driving traffic to your affiliate offers is a multifaceted process that requires a strategic approach, continuous experimentation, and optimization. By implementing a combination of SEO, content marketing, social media marketing, email marketing, and performance analysis, you can attract targeted traffic, engage your audience, and drive conversions effectively. Stay informed about industry trends, adapt to changes in consumer behavior, and focus on delivering value to your audience to achieve sustainable success in affiliate marketing.

Chapter 7:

Converting Visitors into Customers

Converting visitors into customers is the ultimate goal of affiliate marketing. While driving traffic to your affiliate offers is crucial, it's equally important to optimize your conversion process to maximize your revenue potential. In this guide, we'll explore effective strategies and tactics for converting visitors into customers and increasing your affiliate sales.

1. Understanding the Buyer's Journey

Before diving into specific conversion tactics, it's essential to understand the buyer's journey—the process that potential customers go through before making a purchase. The buyer's journey typically consists of three stages:

- **Awareness**: The customer becomes aware of a need or problem that they want to solve.

- **Consideration**: The customer researches and evaluates potential solutions or products to address their need or problem.
- **Decision**: The customer makes a purchase decision based on the information gathered during the consideration stage.

By understanding where your visitors are in the buyer's journey, you can tailor your content and offers to meet their needs and guide them towards making a purchase.

2. Creating Compelling Content

Compelling content is key to engaging your audience and convincing them to take action. Here are some strategies for creating content that drives conversions:

- **Educational Content**: Provide valuable information and insights related to your niche or the products you're promoting. Answer common questions, address pain points, and offer solutions to your audience's problems.

- **Product Reviews**: Write detailed and honest reviews of the products or services you're promoting. Highlight key features, benefits, and drawbacks to help your audience make informed purchasing decisions.

- **Tutorials and How-To Guides**: Create step-by-step tutorials and guides that demonstrate how to use the products or achieve specific outcomes related to your niche. Showcasing practical examples can increase the perceived value of the products and encourage conversions.

- **Case Studies and Success Stories**: Share real-life examples of how the products or services have helped customers solve problems or achieve their goals. Case studies and success stories provide social proof and build trust with your audience.

- **Visual Content**: Incorporate visual elements such as images, infographics, videos, and slideshows to enhance the visual appeal and engagement of your content. Visual content can help communicate complex information more effectively and capture attention.

3. Implementing Conversion Optimization Tactics

Once you've created compelling content, it's time to optimize your website and marketing strategies to convert visitors into customers. Here are some conversion optimization tactics to consider:

- **Clear Call-to-Action (CTA)**: Use clear and compelling calls-to-action (CTAs) to prompt visitors to take the desired action, whether it's making a purchase, signing up for a newsletter, or downloading a resource. Place CTAs strategically throughout your content and make them stand out visually.

- **Optimized Landing Pages**: Create dedicated landing pages for your affiliate offers that are designed to convert visitors into customers. Optimize your landing pages for clarity, relevance, and persuasiveness, and remove any distractions that may detract from the conversion goal.

- **A/B Testing**: Experiment with different variations of your landing pages, CTAs, headlines, and content to identify what resonates best with your audience and drives the highest conversions. Conduct A/B tests and analyze the results to refine your approach over time.

- **Social Proof**: Incorporate social proof elements such as customer testimonials, reviews, ratings, and endorsements to build trust and credibility with your audience. Highlight positive experiences and outcomes to reassure visitors that they're making the right decision.

- **Urgency and Scarcity**: Create a sense of urgency and scarcity to motivate visitors to take action. Use countdown timers, limited-time offers, and low-stock notifications to convey a sense of exclusivity and encourage immediate decision-making.

- **Optimized Forms**: If your conversion process involves forms or opt-in fields, streamline the process by minimizing the number of fields required and optimizing the form layout for ease of use. Use autofill functionality and clear error messages to reduce friction and improve completion rates.

4. **Leveraging Email Marketing**

Email marketing is a powerful tool for nurturing leads, building relationships, and driving conversions. Here's how to leverage email marketing to convert visitors into customers:

- **Lead Magnets**: Offer valuable lead magnets such as ebooks, guides, checklists, or templates in exchange for visitors' email addresses. Use lead magnets to capture leads and initiate the email nurturing process.

- **Automated Email Sequences**: Set up automated email sequences to deliver targeted content, promotions, and recommendations to your subscribers based on their interests and behavior. Use email automation to guide subscribers through the buyer's journey and encourage conversions.

- **Personalization**: Personalize your email content and recommendations based on subscriber preferences, purchase history, and demographic information. Segment your email list and tailor your messaging to each segment to increase relevance and engagement.

- **Promotional Emails**: Send promotional emails featuring exclusive offers, discounts, and incentives to encourage subscribers to make a purchase. Use persuasive copywriting, compelling visuals, and clear calls-to-action to drive conversions directly from your emails.

5. Analyzing and Optimizing Performance

Monitor and analyze the performance of your conversion optimization efforts using web analytics tools, email marketing platforms, and affiliate tracking software. Track key metrics such as conversion rates, click-through rates, open rates, and revenue generated from affiliate sales. Use this data to identify trends, identify areas for improvement, and optimize your conversion strategies accordingly.

- **Conversion Funnel Analysis**: Analyze your conversion funnel to identify potential bottlenecks or drop-off points where visitors are abandoning the conversion process. Optimize each stage of the funnel to reduce friction and improve conversion rates.

- **Multivariate Testing**: Experiment with different combinations of elements within your conversion funnel, such as landing page layouts, CTAs, email subject lines, and offer variations. Conduct multivariate tests to identify the most effective combinations for driving conversions.

- **Customer Feedback**: Gather feedback from your customers and subscribers through surveys, polls, and feedback forms. Use customer insights to understand their needs, preferences, and pain points, and tailor your conversion strategies accordingly.

6. Conclusion

Converting visitors into customers is a multifaceted process that requires a strategic approach, continuous optimization, and a deep understanding of your audience's needs and preferences. By creating compelling content, implementing conversion optimization tactics, leveraging email marketing, and analyzing performance data, you can maximize your affiliate sales and revenue potential. Stay informed about industry trends, experiment with different strategies, and continuously refine your approach to achieve sustainable success in affiliate marketing.

Chapter 8:

Optimizing Your Affiliate Marketing Strategy

Optimizing your affiliate marketing strategy is essential for maximizing your revenue potential and achieving long-term success in the competitive world of affiliate marketing. By continuously refining and improving your approach, you can attract more traffic, convert more visitors into customers, and ultimately, increase your affiliate sales and commissions. In this guide, we'll explore various strategies and tactics for optimizing your affiliate marketing strategy effectively.

1. Conduct Regular Performance Analysis

Regular performance analysis is crucial for identifying strengths, weaknesses, and areas for improvement in your affiliate marketing strategy. Here are some key metrics to monitor and analyze:

- Traffic Sources: Identify the sources of your website or blog traffic, including search engines, social media platforms, referral sites, and direct traffic. Determine which sources drive the most traffic and conversions and allocate resources accordingly.

- **Conversion Rates**: Track conversion rates at each stage of the conversion funnel, from click-through rates on affiliate links to completed purchases. Identify any bottlenecks or drop-off points in the conversion process and implement strategies to address them.

- Earnings per Click (EPC)*: Calculate the earnings per click for each affiliate offer or promotional campaign. Compare the EPC of different offers to identify high-performing opportunities and prioritize them in your promotional efforts.

- **Customer Lifetime Value (CLV)**: Evaluate the lifetime value of your customers to understand the long-term impact of your affiliate marketing efforts. Focus on acquiring and retaining high-value customers who make repeat purchases and generate consistent revenue over time.

2. Test and Experiment with Different Strategies

Experimentation is key to discovering what works best for your audience and niche. Test different strategies, tactics, and approaches to identify what resonates most with your audience and drives the highest results. Here are some areas to experiment with:

- **Content Formats**: Experiment with different types of content, including blog posts, videos, podcasts, infographics, and social media posts. Determine which formats generate the most engagement and conversions and prioritize them in your content strategy.

- **Promotional Channels**: Test different promotional channels, including search engine optimization (SEO), social media marketing, email marketing, influencer partnerships, and paid advertising. Measure the effectiveness of each channel in driving traffic and conversions and allocate resources accordingly.

- **Offer Selection**: Experiment with different affiliate offers, products, and merchants within your niche. Test offers with different commission structures, pricing models, and promotional resources to identify the most lucrative opportunities for your audience.

- **Call-to-Action (CTA) Variations**: Test different CTAs, button colors, text placements, and messaging to optimize conversion rates. Experiment with urgency-inducing phrases, benefit-driven language, and personalized CTAs to encourage action from your audience.

*3. Optimize Your Website and Content

Your website and content play a crucial role in attracting visitors, engaging your audience, and driving conversions. Here are some strategies for optimizing your website and content:

- **Mobile Optimization**: Ensure that your website is optimized for mobile devices to provide a seamless user experience across all devices. Use responsive design, fast-loading pages, and mobile-friendly navigation to accommodate mobile users effectively.

- **Search Engine Optimization (SEO)**: Optimize your website and content for search engines to improve visibility and attract organic traffic. Conduct keyword research, optimize meta tags and headings, and create high-quality, keyword-rich content to rank higher in search engine results.

- **User Experience (UX) Design**: Enhance the user experience of your website by improving navigation, layout, and usability. Make it easy for visitors to find information, navigate between pages, and complete desired actions, such as signing up for newsletters or making purchases.

- **Content Quality and Relevance**: Create high-quality, informative, and engaging content that resonates with your audience and provides value. Focus on addressing your audience's needs, solving their problems, and delivering actionable insights that inspire action.

4. Build Relationships and Trust

Building relationships and trust with your audience is essential for establishing credibility, fostering loyalty, and driving repeat business. Here are some strategies for building relationships and trust:

- **Authenticity and Transparency**: Be authentic and transparent in your interactions with your audience. Share personal stories, experiences, and insights to connect with your audience on a human level and build trust over time.

- **Engagement and Interaction**: Engage with your audience regularly through comments, messages, and social media interactions. Respond to questions, address concerns, and show appreciation for feedback to demonstrate your commitment to customer satisfaction.

- **Value-Driven Content**: Focus on delivering value to your audience through informative, educational, and entertaining content. Provide actionable advice, practical tips, and exclusive insights that demonstrate your expertise and benefit your audience.

- **Customer Support and Service**: Provide exceptional customer support and service to address customer inquiries, resolve issues, and ensure a positive experience. Offer multiple communication channels, such as email, live chat, and social media, to accommodate customer preferences.

*5. Stay Informed and Adapt to Changes

The affiliate marketing landscape is constantly evolving, with new trends, technologies, and regulations emerging regularly. Stay informed about industry developments, changes in consumer behavior, and updates to affiliate programs and policies. Here are some ways to stay informed:

- **Industry News and Updates**: Follow industry news sources, blogs, forums, and social media accounts to stay up-to-date on the latest trends and developments in affiliate marketing.

- **Networking and Collaboration**: Join affiliate marketing communities, forums, and networking groups to connect with other affiliates, share insights, and learn from each other's experiences. Collaborate on joint ventures, partnerships, and promotions to expand your reach and grow your affiliate business collaboratively.

- **Continuous Learning and Education**: Invest in your ongoing learning and education by attending webinars, workshops, conferences, and online courses related to affiliate marketing. Stay abreast of best practices, emerging strategies, and industry innovations to remain competitive and adapt to changes proactively.

- **Adaptation and Flexibility**: Be flexible and adaptable in your approach to affiliate marketing. Be willing to experiment with new strategies, pivot when necessary, and adjust your tactics based on evolving market conditions, consumer preferences, and industry trends.

***6. Monitor and Track Key Metrics**

Monitoring and tracking key metrics is essential for evaluating the effectiveness of your optimization efforts and identifying areas for improvement. Here are some key metrics to monitor:

- **Conversion Rates*: Track conversion rates for your affiliate offers, landing pages, and promotional campaigns. Identify which offers and strategies are driving the highest conversion rates and allocate resources accordingly.

- **Return on Investment (ROI)**: Calculate the return on investment for your marketing activities by comparing the revenue generated from affiliate sales to the costs associated with acquiring traffic and promoting offers. Focus on optimizing campaigns with the highest ROI to maximize profitability.

- **Customer Acquisition Cost (CAC)**: Determine the cost of acquiring each new customer by dividing your total marketing expenses by the number of new customers acquired. Aim to minimize your

CAC while maximizing customer lifetime value to achieve sustainable growth.

- **Engagement Metrics**: Monitor engagement metrics such as click-through rates, time on site, bounce rates, and social media engagement. Analyze engagement data to understand how visitors are interacting with your content and identify opportunities for improvement.

7. Conclusion

Optimizing your affiliate marketing strategy is an ongoing process that requires continuous learning, experimentation, and adaptation. By conducting regular performance analysis, testing different strategies, optimizing your website and content, building relationships and trust with your audience, staying informed about industry trends, and monitoring key metrics, you can maximize your revenue potential and achieve long-term success as an affiliate marketer. Remember to prioritize providing value to your audience, delivering exceptional customer experiences, and maintaining transparency and authenticity in your interactions. With dedication, persistence, and a strategic approach, you can optimize your affiliate marketing strategy to drive sustainable growth and profitability in the competitive affiliate marketing landscape.

Chapter 9:

Legal and Ethical Considerations in Affiliate Marketing

Affiliate marketing offers numerous opportunities for earning income online, but it also comes with legal and ethical responsibilities that affiliates must adhere to. From compliance with regulatory requirements to maintaining transparency and honesty with your audience, understanding and following legal and ethical guidelines is essential for building a successful and sustainable affiliate marketing business. In this guide, we'll explore key legal and ethical considerations that every affiliate marketer should be aware of.

1. Compliance with Regulatory Requirements

Affiliate marketers must comply with various regulatory requirements imposed by government agencies and industry organizations to ensure fair and transparent business practices. Here are some important regulations and guidelines to consider:

- Federal Trade Commission (FTC) Guidelines*: The FTC requires affiliate marketers to disclose their relationship with advertisers and disclose any material connections, such as affiliate links, endorsements, or sponsored content. Disclosures should be clear, conspicuous, and prominently displayed to avoid misleading consumers.

- **General Data Protection Regulation (GDPR)**: If you target users in the European Union (EU) or collect personal data from EU residents, you must comply with the GDPR's requirements for data protection and privacy. This includes obtaining explicit consent for data collection, providing transparent privacy policies, and implementing security measures to protect user data.

- California Consumer Privacy Act (CCPA): If you target users in California or collect personal information from California residents, you must comply with the CCPA's requirements for consumer privacy rights, including the right to opt-out of data sharing and the right to access and delete personal information.

- CAN-SPAM Act*: The CAN-SPAM Act regulates commercial email communications and requires affiliate marketers to include accurate header information, provide clear and conspicuous unsubscribe links, and honor opt-out requests promptly.

- **Advertising Standards Authority (ASA)**: In the United Kingdom, the ASA regulates advertising standards and requires affiliate marketers to ensure that their advertising is legal, decent, honest, and truthful. Affiliates must avoid making false or misleading claims and must be able to substantiate any claims made in their promotional materials.

2. Transparency and Disclosure

Transparency and disclosure are fundamental principles of ethical affiliate marketing. Affiliates must be transparent about their relationship with advertisers and disclose any material connections or incentives that may influence their recommendations or endorsements. Here are some best practices for transparency and disclosure:

- **Clear and Conspicuous Disclosures**: Disclosures should be clear, conspicuous, and prominently displayed in close proximity to affiliate links or endorsements. Use language that is easy to understand and avoid technical jargon or legalistic terms.

- Disclosure Formats*: Disclosures can take various formats, including text disclosures (e.g., "This post contains affiliate links"), visual disclosures (e.g., "Sponsored" labels on images), or audio disclosures (e.g., verbal disclosures in podcasts or videos). Choose the format that best suits the medium and context of your content.

- **Consistent Disclosure Practices**: Establish consistent disclosure practices across all your marketing channels and content formats to ensure compliance and avoid confusion. Use standardized disclosure language and placement to maintain transparency and build trust with your audience.

3. Honesty and Integrity

Honesty and integrity are essential ethical principles that every affiliate marketer should uphold. Building trust with your audience requires honesty, authenticity, and transparency in your marketing efforts. Here are some tips for maintaining honesty and integrity:

70

- **Authentic Recommendations**: Only promote products or services that you genuinely believe in and would recommend to your friends or family. Avoid promoting low-quality or scammy products solely for the sake of earning commissions.

- **Full Disclosure of Affiliation**: Disclose your affiliation with advertisers and any incentives or compensation received for promoting their products. Be upfront and transparent about your financial interests and avoid misleading or deceptive marketing practices.

- **Unbiased Reviews and Recommendations**: Provide balanced and unbiased reviews and recommendations that highlight both the pros and cons of the products or services you're promoting. Offer honest assessments based on your personal experiences and insights.

*4. Respect for Consumer Privacy

Respecting consumer privacy is critical in affiliate marketing, especially in light of increasing concerns about data protection and online privacy. Affiliates must handle consumer data responsibly and comply with applicable privacy laws and regulations. Here are some privacy considerations to keep in mind:

- **Data Collection and Consent**: Obtain explicit consent from users before collecting any personal data, such as email addresses or browsing behavior. Clearly communicate how you will use their data and provide options for opting out or withdrawing consent.

- **Data Security**: Implement robust security measures to protect consumer data from unauthorized access, disclosure, or misuse. Use encryption, firewalls, and other security technologies to safeguard sensitive information and prevent data breaches.

- **Transparency in Data Practices**: Be transparent about your data collection and processing practices by providing clear and concise privacy policies that outline what data you collect, how you use it, and how users can exercise their privacy rights.

5. Avoiding Deceptive Practices

Affiliate marketers must avoid engaging in deceptive or misleading practices that could harm consumers or damage their reputation. Deceptive practices undermine trust and credibility, leading to negative consequences for both affiliates and advertisers. Here are some common deceptive practices to avoid:

- **False Claims and Guarantees**: Avoid making false or exaggerated claims about the benefits or outcomes of the products or services you're promoting. Be honest and realistic about what users can expect and avoid promising guaranteed results or outcomes.

- Fake Reviews and Testimonials: Do not fabricate or manipulate reviews, testimonials, or social proof to deceive consumers. Only use genuine testimonials from real customers who have used the products or services and disclose any incentives or compensation received for endorsements.

- Bait-and-Switch Tactics: Do not use bait-and-switch tactics to lure consumers with misleading offers or promotions. Ensure that your marketing messages accurately reflect the terms and conditions of the offers and deliver on the promises made to consumers.

6. Conclusion

Legal and ethical considerations are paramount in affiliate marketing, and adherence to regulatory requirements and ethical guidelines is essential for building trust with your audience, maintaining credibility, and avoiding potential legal issues. By complying with applicable laws and regulations, maintaining transparency and disclosure, upholding honesty and integrity, respecting consumer privacy, and avoiding deceptive practices, affiliate marketers can create a positive and ethical affiliate marketing ecosystem that benefits both consumers and advertisers.
.

Chapter 10:

Case Studies and Success Stories in Affiliate Marketing

Case studies and success stories provide valuable insights into the strategies, tactics, and experiences of affiliate marketers who have achieved notable success in the industry. By examining real-life examples of affiliate marketing campaigns, partnerships, and achievements, aspiring affiliates can learn from the successes and challenges of others and apply proven strategies to their own affiliate marketing endeavors. In this guide, we'll explore several case studies and success stories that highlight different approaches to affiliate marketing and showcase the diverse paths to success in the affiliate marketing landscape.

1. **Pat Flynn - Smart Passive Income**

Pat Flynn is a renowned affiliate marketer and the founder of Smart Passive Income, a popular blog and podcast dedicated to helping people build successful online businesses. One of Pat's most notable affiliate marketing successes is his promotion of Bluehost, a web hosting service. Through in-depth tutorials, guides, and case studies, Pat demonstrated how to start a blog and set up a website using Bluehost, earning significant affiliate commissions in the process. By providing valuable content and transparently disclosing his affiliate relationships, Pat built trust with his audience and generated substantial revenue through affiliate marketing.

Key Takeaways:
- Provide value through educational content: By creating comprehensive tutorials and guides, Pat addressed his audience's needs and helped them achieve their goals, while also promoting affiliate products.
- Be transparent about affiliate relationships: Pat openly disclosed his affiliate relationship with Bluehost and other companies, establishing trust with his audience and maintaining transparency in his marketing efforts.

*2. Michelle Schroeder-Gardner - Making Sense of Cents

Michelle Schroeder-Gardner is a personal finance blogger and affiliate marketer who has achieved remarkable success through her blog, Making Sense of Cents. Michelle's affiliate marketing strategy revolves around promoting financial products and services that align with her audience's interests and needs. One of Michelle's most successful affiliate partnerships is with Personal Capital, a financial planning and investment management platform. Through detailed reviews, comparisons, and testimonials, Michelle educated her audience about the benefits of Personal Capital and generated significant affiliate income from referrals.

Key Takeaways:
- Understand your audience's needs: Michelle identified her audience's interest in personal finance and tailored her affiliate marketing efforts to promote relevant products and services.
- Provide valuable insights and recommendations: Michelle's thorough reviews and testimonials helped her audience make informed decisions about financial products and services, leading to higher conversion rates and affiliate commissions.

3. Wirecutter - Product Recommendations and Reviews

Wirecutter is a product review website owned by The New York Times Company that generates revenue through affiliate marketing. Wirecutter's affiliate marketing strategy focuses on providing comprehensive product recommendations and reviews across a wide range of categories, including tech gadgets, home appliances, and outdoor gear. By conducting rigorous testing and research, Wirecutter produces in-depth reviews and comparison guides that help consumers make informed purchasing decisions. Wirecutter earns affiliate commissions from retailers like Amazon when readers purchase products through their affiliate links.

*Key Takeaways:
- Focus on thorough research and testing: Wirecutter's commitment to providing unbiased and accurate product recommendations has earned the trust of its audience and established it as a leading authority in product reviews.
- Diversify affiliate partnerships: By partnering with multiple retailers and affiliate programs, Wirecutter maximizes its revenue potential and reduces dependency on any single affiliate program or advertiser.

4. Authority Hacker - Niche Authority Sites

Authority Hacker is a website and podcast that provides resources, tutorials, and case studies for building authority niche websites and affiliate marketing businesses. The founders, Gael Breton and Mark Webster, have achieved success by creating niche authority sites in various industries, such as health and wellness, technology, and personal finance. Through keyword research, content creation, and SEO optimization, Authority Hacker builds profitable niche websites that attract targeted traffic and generate affiliate income through product recommendations and affiliate promotions.

Key Takeaways:
- Focus on niche authority sites: Authority Hacker's strategy revolves around building niche authority sites that target specific audiences and industries, allowing them to establish credibility and attract highly relevant traffic.
- Invest in SEO and content marketing: Authority Hacker emphasizes the importance of SEO and content marketing for driving organic traffic to niche authority sites and maximizing affiliate revenue potential.

Conclusion

These case studies and success stories illustrate the diverse strategies, tactics, and approaches to affiliate marketing that have led to notable success for various affiliates and businesses. From providing valuable content and transparently disclosing affiliate relationships to understanding audience needs and leveraging niche authority sites, these examples showcase the principles and practices that underpin successful affiliate marketing campaigns. By studying these case studies and success stories, aspiring affiliates can gain valuable insights and inspiration for building their own successful affiliate marketing businesses.

Conclusion:

Navigating the World of Affiliate Marketing

Affiliate marketing offers boundless opportunities for individuals and businesses to generate income online, but success in this competitive landscape requires a combination of strategy, diligence, and ethical conduct. Throughout this guide, we've explored the multifaceted world of affiliate marketing, covering a wide range of topics, from getting started as a beginner to optimizing your strategy for long-term success. Let's recap some of the key points and takeaways:

1. Getting Started:
- Begin by understanding the fundamentals of affiliate marketing, including how it works, the roles of affiliates and merchants, and the various affiliate marketing models.
- Choose a niche that aligns with your interests, expertise, and audience's needs, and conduct thorough research to identify profitable opportunities within your chosen niche.
- Select reputable affiliate programs and platforms, and familiarize yourself with their terms of service,

commission structures, and promotional guidelines.

2. **Building Your Presence:**
- Establish a strong online presence through a blog, website, or social media channels, and create high-quality, engaging content that provides value to your audience.
- Optimize your website for search engines (SEO) to attract organic traffic and improve your visibility in search engine results pages.
- Leverage email marketing, social media marketing, and other promotional channels to expand your reach and attract targeted traffic to your affiliate offers.

3. **Monetizing Your Traffic:**

- Choose affiliate products and services that are relevant to your audience's interests and needs, and promote them authentically and transparently.
- Implement various monetization strategies, including affiliate links, banner ads, sponsored content, and product reviews, to diversify your revenue streams and maximize your earning potential.
- Continuously analyze and optimize your conversion process to increase your affiliate sales

and commissions, and experiment with different tactics and approaches to identify what works best for your audience.

4. Legal and Ethical Considerations:
- Adhere to regulatory requirements and industry guidelines, including FTC regulations, GDPR compliance, and advertising standards, to ensure fair and transparent business practices.
- Maintain transparency and disclosure in your marketing efforts by clearly disclosing your affiliate relationships and any incentives or compensation received for promoting products or services.
- Uphold honesty, integrity, and respect for consumer privacy in all your affiliate marketing activities, and avoid engaging in deceptive or misleading practices that could harm consumers or damage your reputation.

5. Learning from Success Stories:
- Study case studies and success stories from successful affiliate marketers, such as Pat Flynn, Michelle Schroeder-Gardner, Wirecutter, and Authority Hacker, to gain insights into their strategies, tactics, and approaches.
- Learn from their successes and challenges, and apply proven strategies and best practices to your own affiliate marketing endeavors.

- Remember that success in affiliate marketing is not guaranteed overnight and requires dedication, persistence, and continuous learning and adaptation.

In conclusion, affiliate marketing offers unparalleled opportunities for individuals and businesses to generate income online, but success requires a strategic approach, ethical conduct, and a commitment to providing value to your audience. By following the principles and practices outlined in this guide, you can navigate the complexities of the affiliate marketing landscape, build a successful affiliate marketing business, and achieve your financial and entrepreneurial goals.

Remember that affiliate marketing is a journey, and success may not come overnight. Stay patient, persistent, and focused on delivering value to your audience, and you'll be well on your way to building a thriving affiliate marketing business that generates sustainable income and long-term success.

As you embark on your affiliate marketing journey, keep in mind that the principles of integrity, transparency, and authenticity will serve as your guiding lights. Stay true to your values, build trust with your audience, and always prioritize providing value and solving their problems. With dedication, perseverance, and a commitment to ethical conduct, you can achieve success and make a positive impact in the world of affiliate marketing.

Now, armed with the knowledge and insights gained from this guide, it's time to take action and embark on your own affiliate marketing journey. Whether you're a beginner just starting out or an experienced marketer looking to optimize your strategy, remember that success is within reach if you're willing to put in the effort and stay true to your principles.

Here's to your success in affiliate marketing!

Thanks for reading

www.ingramcontent.com/pod-product-compliance
Lightning Source LLC
Chambersburg PA
CBHW050234230526
45470CB00005B/1955

LA GUIA ESSENCIAL DEL FOTÒGRAF
40 CONSELLS I ETIQUETA PER A PRINCIPIANTS